JUL 2013

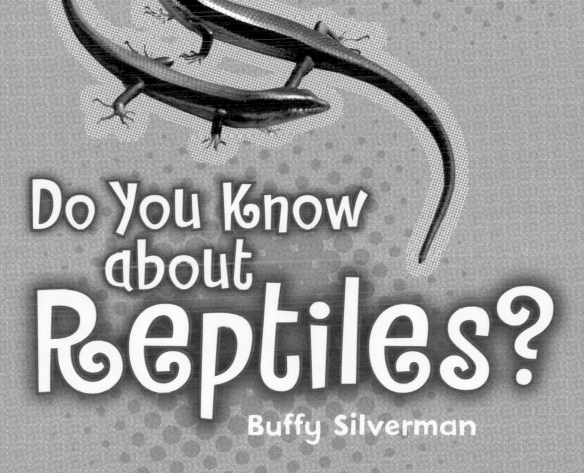

LIGHTNING BOLT BOOKS™

Do You Know about Reptiles?

Buffy Silverman

Lerner Publications Company

Minneapolis

To Gabi
and her mom

Lerner Publications Company
A division of Lerner Publishing Group, Inc.
241 First Avenue North
Minneapolis, MN 55401 U.S.A.

Website address: www.lernerbooks.com

Library of Congress Cataloging-in-Publication Data

Silverman, Buffy.
        Do you know about reptiles? / by Buffy Silverman.
            p.   cm. — (Lightning bolt books™ — Meet the animal groups)
        Includes index.
        ISBN 978-0-8225-7542-9 (lib. bdg. : alk. paper)
        1. Reptiles — Juvenile literature. I. Title.
    QL644.2.S557 2010
    597.9—dc22   2008050759

Manufactured in the United States of America
1 2 3 4 5 6 — BP — 15 14 13 12 11 10

Contents

What is a Reptile?

An alligator dives underwater to catch a fish. A sidewinder springs forward and bites a mouse. A wood turtle chews berries in a field. A horned lizard gobbles ants. Alligators, snakes, turtles, and lizards look very different. They eat different foods. But all are reptiles.

This wood turtle lives in a stream in the forest.

An alligator looks for food in the water.

Reptiles are animals with dry, scaly skin. Their thick scales protect their bodies. Scales hold in water too. Scaly skin lets some reptiles live in dry places.

A skink has smooth scales.

Snakes have wide scales on their bellies. Scales help them glide across the ground. Can you see the scales on this snake's belly?

A snapping turtle has small scales on its neck. Large scales cover its shell.

Can you see the large scales on this snapping turtle?

A turtle's backbone is part of its shell. Animals with backbones are called vertebrates. Reptiles are vertebrates.

Turtles have backbones inside their shells.

Look at the snake slide over the ground. Its backbone is made up of hundreds of small bones. Long backbones let snakes twist and turn.

Snakes use their long backbones to move.

A crocodile has a strong backbone. The crocodile runs on land. It swishes its powerful tail to swim underwater. The crocodile swims to the surface to breathe. All reptiles breathe air. They breathe with lungs.

Crocodiles have backbones. They breathe air.

Staying Warm, Cooling Off

A crocodile basks on a sunny log. The sun warms its body. Reptiles cannot make their own body heat. They are ectotherms. They get warm or cool from their surroundings.

This crocodile warms its body in the sun.

An iguana warms up on a rock in the desert.

13

Most reptiles live on or near land in warm places. What do reptiles do when it is cold? Many find safe places to sleep. They hibernate.

Every fall, prairie rattlesnakes travel to the same den. They hibernate there during winter.

Desert tortoises dig holes underground. At night, the desert cools off. Underground holes stay warmer than the cold night air. The holes also stay cool when the hot sun shines.

A desert tortoise stays cool in a shady hole.

staying safe

Some reptiles are hard to find. The lizard's spotted skin blends in with the speckled rock. Its camouflage keeps it safe.

Can you spot the granite lizard on this rock?

How do other reptiles stay safe? A skink can drop its tail if an animal grabs it. The skink runs away and leaves behind its wiggling tail. The skink will grow a new tail.

This skink dropped its tail. It is growing a new tail.

A box turtle pulls in its head, tail, and legs. It clamps its shell shut. A hungry fox sniffs the turtle. But the fox cannot bite through the turtle's tough shell.

A box turtle hides in its shell. The shell keeps it safe.

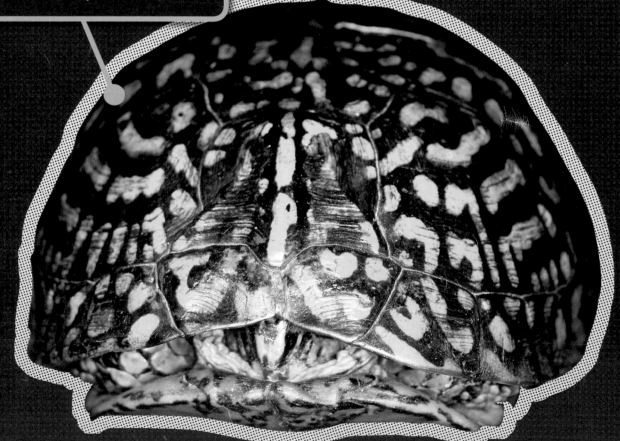

A rattlesnake shakes its rattle. The sound warns enemies to stay away.

Can you see the rattle on this rattlesnake?

Green iguanas
are reptiles.

Eggs and Babies

Most reptiles lay eggs on land. Green iguanas live in trees. They climb down to dig a nest and lay eggs.

Green iguanas lay more than twenty eggs at a time.

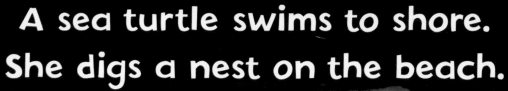

A sea turtle swims to shore.
She digs a nest on the beach.

She lays round eggs with rubbery shells. Tiny turtles hatch from the eggs.

A sea turtle lays eggs in her nest. Then she covers the eggs with sand.

The baby sea turtles crawl to the water. Birds, raccoons, and fish eat many of them.

A female garter snake carries her babies inside her body. She can give birth to forty babies or more. The babies take care of themselves.

Baby garter snakes crawl over their mother and stay near her. But she does not feed or protect them.

Most reptiles do not stay with their young. But a mother alligator cares for her babies. She lays her eggs in a muddy nest.

A mother alligator protects her eggs.

Two months later, the babies hatch. The mother hears them yip. She leads them to water and keeps them safe. Soon they will hunt on their own.

Baby alligators stay with their mother. The mother chases away enemies.

Reptile Records

Largest lizard: The Komodo dragon can grow 10 feet (3 meters) long and weigh 200 pounds (91 kilograms). With its sixty teeth, it can tear apart pigs and deer.

Littlest lizard: The world's smallest reptile is the dwarf gecko. It is so tiny that it can curl up on a small coin.

Longest snake: In 1912, a python in Indonesia was measured at 33 feet (10 m) long. That is as long as a school bus!

Oldest living animal: The oldest known tortoise lived at least 188 years. Tortoises often live over 100 years.

Racing reptile: A spiny-tailed iguana can run 21 miles (34 kilometers) per hour.

Flying reptiles: No reptiles can actually fly. But some snakes and lizards glide through the air. The flying dragon stretches out flaps of skin on the side of its body. With these "wings," it can glide 25 feet (8m) from tree to tree.

Weirdest lizard: A Texas horned lizard blows up like a balloon if an enemy nears. If the lizard is still frightened, it squirts blood from its eyes.

Glossary

bask: lie in the sun

camouflage: coloring that helps an animal blend in with its surroundings

ectotherm: an animal whose body temperature changes when the temperature of its surroundings changes

hibernate: to be inactive and sleep

lung: an organ used for breathing

reptile: an animal with scaly skin that has a backbone and breathes air with lungs. Most reptiles lay eggs. Crocodiles, snakes, turtles, and lizards are reptiles.

scale: a tough, hard plate that covers and protects a reptile's skin

vertebrate: an animal with a backbone

Further Reading

Holland, Simon. *Reptiles*. New York: DK Publishing, 2002.

Howell, Catherine Herbert. *Reptiles & Amphibians*. Washington, DC: National Geographic Society, 1993.

Jenkins, Martin. *Chameleons Are Cool*. Somerville, MA: Candlewick Press, 1998.

Lauber, Patricia. *Snakes Are Hunters*. New York: HarperCollins, 1988.

Wilson, Hannah. *Life-Size Reptiles*. New York: Sterling Publishing, 2007.

Winner, Cherie. *Everything Reptile: What Kids Really Want to Know about Reptiles*. Chanhassen, MN: NorthWord Books for Young Readers, 2004.

Reptile Printouts—EnchantedLearning.com
http://www.enchantedlearning.com/subjects/reptiles/printouts.shtml

Reptiles and Amphibians for Kids—Smithsonian National Zoological Park
http://nationalzoo.si.edu/Animals/ReptilesAmphibians/ForKids

Index

Photo Acknowledgments

The images in this book are used with the permission of: © Kenneth Andrew Valles/ Dreamstime.com, p. 1; © Uros Ravbar/Dreamstime.com, p. 2; © Papilio/Alamy, p. 4; © Shai Eynav/SuperStock, p. 5; © Dorling Kindersley/Getty Images, p. 6; © iStockphoto. com/John Pitcher, p. 7; © age fotostock/SuperStock, pp. 8, 19, 23, 27; © Tom Ulrich/ Visuals Unlimited, Inc., p. 9; © Paul Chesley/Stone/Getty Images, p. 10; © Gert Vrey/ Dreamstime.com, p. 11; © Roman Shiyanov-Fotolia.com, p. 12; © Ernest Manewal/ SuperStock, p. 13; © Tom McHugh/Photo Researchers, Inc., p. 14; © Jeff Foott/Dcom/ DRK PHOTO, p. 15; © Chris Mattison/FLPA, p. 16; © Joseph T. & Suzanne L. Collins/ Photo Researchers, Inc., p. 17; © Scott Camazine/Photo Researchers, Inc., p. 18; © Peter Llewellyn/FLPA, p. 20; © E.R. Degginger/Photo Researchers, Inc., p. 21; © Kelvin Aitken/ Alamy, p. 22; © Rene Frederick/Digital Vision/Getty Images, p. 24; © Robert Folz/ Visuals Unlimited, Inc., p. 25; © Mike Brown/Dreamstime.com, p. 26; © Joe McDonald/ Visuals Unlimited, Inc., p. 28; © Bruce Coleman Inc./Alamy, p. 29; © Johnbell/ Dreamstime.com, p. 30.

Front cover: © Norbert Wu/Science Faction/Getty Images (left); © Photodisc/Getty Images (right both).